Animal Habitats

The Ant on the Ground

Text by
Linda Losito

Photographs by
Oxford Scientific Films

Gareth Stevens Publishing
Milwaukee

Contents

Note: The use of capital letters for an ant's name indicates that it is a *species* of ant (for example, Australian Honeypot Ant). The use of a lowercase, or small, letter means that it is a member of a larger *group* of ants.

Carpenter ants from North America eating a dead tent caterpillar.

This wood ant is collecting fresh nest material.

Ants and where they live

Ants are found in almost every part of the world, in many different kinds of *habitats*. They live wherever there is a supply of food for them to eat. You will find them in the woods, in mountain areas, in deserts, on the coast, and even in busy cities. Only the icy snowfields of the North and South poles do not have any ant colonies, because it is too cold for them.

Most ants live on or under the ground. They build their nests in the soil, often under stones or logs. The nest is where the young are reared. Of course, you often see them on the surface, too, scurrying along "ant trails" or up and down plant stems in a constant search for food. Some tropical ants even build their nests up in the trees.

Ants are insects and, along with bees and wasps, belong to a group called the Hymenoptera. This Greek word means that all the insects in this group have transparent wings, unlike the scaly wings of butterflies. Only the mating adult ants have wings. Swarms of these "flying ants" are a common sight in midsummer, often squashed underfoot on the hot pavement.

In our gardens and yards, ants live in underground nests, so we are not always aware of them. But we could not do without them. Ants are some of nature's most important "garbage collectors," carrying huge quantities of dead leaves, animals, and insects down into the soil for food. If you accidentally step on an ant, within minutes its body will have been picked up and carried off by another ant. The goodness locked up in all this dead matter finds its way back to the roots of plants that use it for growth. Ants are also good for the soil because they continually tunnel through it, breaking it up into fine crumbs. This lets in air and allows excess water to drain away, so plant roots can "breathe."

Weaver ants pull the edges of leaves together to make a nest.

Ants around the world

Ants are probably the most successful group of insects in the world. They are found on all continents and islands, and in every habitat from the hot dry deserts to humid rain forests. They are probably so successful because they live together in colonies and cooperate in tasks like food gathering and nest building. The colony may be quite small with less than a dozen *workers*, or very large with several million ants. But no ant lives alone.

There are about 10,000 *species* of ants living around the world. They are especially numerous in tropical regions. In South America there are more ants than any other living creature. Indeed, if the total weight of all ants and termites were added together, they would weigh more than half the weight of all the other animals combined!

In the tropics, many ants nest up in the trees. Some build a nest like those of wasps made out of papery chewed wood pulp. These nests may be occupied for twenty years and grow to a great size. African weaver ants make their nests out of living leaves. The leaf edges are drawn together by worker ants using their feet and jaws. The ants then firmly glue the edges together using sticky silk produced from the head glands of an ant *larva*.

Australian Honeypot Ant workers become storage vessels for the honeydew gathered by other ants.

Some ants have developed very specialized lifestyles to suit the extreme conditions in which they live. Deserts have times of plenty and scarcity, so the animals that live there have to store food when it is available. The Honeypot Ants of Australia use their own workers as living storage bottles. A foraging worker returns to the underground nest with a crop full of *honeydew* gathered from aphids and passes it to another worker. Unlike bees, ants do not store food in wax cells, so the worker holds it inside its own crop. As more foragers return, the storage ants slowly fill up with honeydew until their greatly swollen *abdomens* are completely round. They hang upside down from the roof of the nest, unable to move. Throughout the season of scarcity, the other ants take droplets of food from the mouths of the storage ants until they return to their normal size.

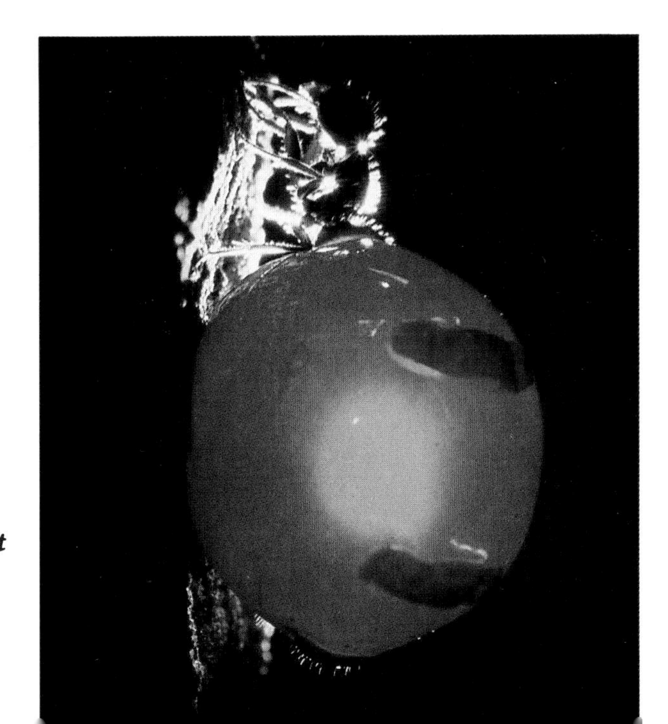

The body of this Australian Honeypot Ant is completely swollen with stored honeydew.

The ant's body

Look closely at an ant. You will see that, like all insects, its body has three main parts: the head, *thorax*, and abdomen. The skeleton is on the outside of the body. It is called an *exoskeleton*, and is made of a tough substance called chitin. This chitin protects the soft parts of the ant's body and supports the muscles.

The ant's head carries the mouthparts, a pair of "feelers" or *antennae*, and two *compound eyes*. The mouth has toothed jaws for biting and chewing. Behind the jaws are two pairs of short *palps*, which are used for touching and tasting. The antennae are also sensitive to touch, but are mainly used for smelling. They are important because ants live in a world of smells.

The compound eyes are divided into many sections called facets. Each facet works like a separate eye and provides just one part of the image that the ant sees. The smaller the number of facets, the poorer the ant's eyesight. The workers of some species, like the driver ants of Africa, have no eyes at all. They find their way around using their antennae and sense organs in their feet. Some ants also have three simple eyes, or *ocelli*, in a triangle on top of the head. These simple eyes are sensitive to light and enable ants to find their direction using sunlight.

The ant's body is divided into three main sections with a narrow waist in between the thorax and the abdomen.

Army ants have a special "soldier" caste. They have huge jaws, and their job is to protect the smaller workers.

The thorax bears six legs and, in mating adults, two pairs of wings. Thus, most of the muscles in an ant's body are found in the thorax; they are attached to the exoskeleton through which they power the legs and wings. Each leg has several separate sections that are hinged together to allow flexible movement. At the end of each foot are two hooked claws that help the ant grip as it runs up and down flat surfaces. Males and young *queen* ants are winged and mate in the air. The queen sheds her wings when she lands after the mating flight.

Between the thorax and abdomen, ants have a narrow "waist" with bumps called nodes. The abdomen contains the ant's gut and waste-disposal systems. In male ants the abdomen contains the testes, which make *sperm*, while females have *ovaries,* which make eggs. The queens and workers of some species have a stinger at the tip of the abdomen which they use to inject poison into *prey* and enemies.

Ants come in many different shapes and sizes. The familiar Black Ant is only about half an inch (13 mm) long and is quite harmless. But the fearsome bulldog ants of Australia are three times as big, with large jaws and a powerful sting.

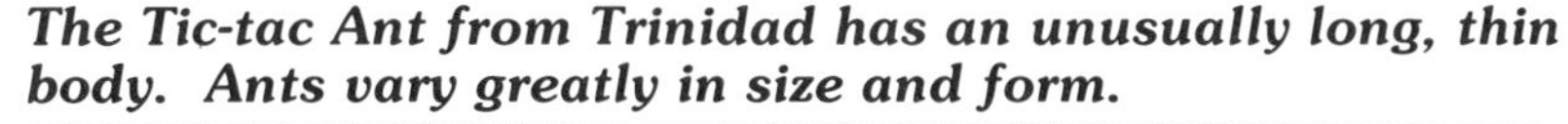

The Tic-tac Ant from Trinidad has an unusually long, thin body. Ants vary greatly in size and form.

This army ant queen has a large abdomen swollen with eggs. She is much bigger than the worker ant on top of her.

The life of the colony

Like many bees and wasps, ants are called "social insects" because they live together in family groups. Large colonies consist of one or more fertile females called queens, plus thousands or millions of sterile female workers and several hundred males.

The queen is at least one-and-a-half times bigger than a typical worker, and she may live for ten to fifteen years. Once she has mated, she does not leave the nest again, and she relies on the busy workers to feed her. She is really just an egg-laying machine and finds it difficult to move around with her large bloated abdomen. The workers lick a chemical called *queen substance* from her body and pass it around the nest from mouth to mouth. This tells them that the queen is fit and healthy.

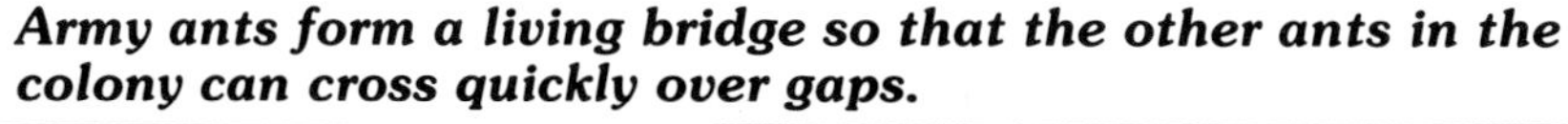

Army ants form a living bridge so that the other ants in the colony can cross quickly over gaps.

It's a trap! These ants are lying in wait to ambush female fungus gnats as they come in to lay their eggs.

Although the worker ants are female, they do not mate. But they do lay eggs occasionally, and these unfertilized eggs hatch into males. Most of the workers' energy goes into looking after the queen and sister workers. They have a short life span and are constantly replaced as new eggs hatch.

There are different sizes of workers. The smaller ones tend to stay in the nest, looking after the young and clearing out waste. The larger workers go out and forage for food. As they return, some species of ants lay a scent trail of chemicals called *pheromones*. This helps other ants in the colony to find the food. Guards at the nest entrance "smell" all returning ants with their antennae, and only those with the right nest smell are allowed in. Any sweet juices that the ants collect on their foraging trips are partially digested and then passed to the mouth of a nest ant. The nest ants then feed it to the queens and to the hungry young larvae, although they also take some for themselves. Worker ants also mend and build new parts of the nest. Some tropical ants have especially large workers called "soldiers" with fearsome pincerlike jaws. The soldiers protect the colony from enemies.

Male ants are only produced in fairly small numbers because they are not so important. They do not work and have to be fed by their sisters. They are only needed when there is a new queen to be mated. They do not live very long, and they die soon after mating.

The Mulga Ant of central Australia builds circular walls around its nest entrances.

Nest building

Everybody needs a home, and ants are no exception. There are few species which do not build a nest. Some ants make temporary nests in hollow plant stems, nuts, or even empty snail shells. Others build complex structures which last for years.

African driver ants are ferocious hunters, constantly moving from place to place in search of food. They only make temporary camps, or "bivouacs," where they stay for a few days or weeks. The workers excavate tunnels in the ground to give protection to the larvae which they carry with them. Army ants from South America have a similar lifestyle, but they usually stay for just a single night in one place. The ants cluster together in a dense mass in a hollow or under a log. They protect the queen and larvae in the center of the mass.

Most ants nest in the ground. They build a complicated system of underground tunnels by digging out soil with their jaws. Each soil particle is carried to the surface and dumped away from the nest entrance. Some of the excavated tunnels are used as "brood chambers" where the young are raised.

In warmer months, European red ants pile any soil they have excavated into a large mound. They continue their tunnels up into this mound. It catches the sun's warmth and heats up more quickly than the ground. The ants carry their larvae into the mound during the day because the extra warmth speeds up their development.

Wood ants thatch their large, sprawling mounds with pine needles or twigs. This provides excellent insulation and helps keep out the rain. These mounds heat up quickly, so the ants build ventilation "doors" to let some of the heat escape; in cold weather the ants plug them with dead plant material.

One species of ant from Africa has given up building its own nests and lives instead in the nests of termites, feeding on their eggs and larvae. The blind worker ants rarely venture outside of the termite mound. These minute workers are less than 1/16 inch (2 mm) long, which is a great many times smaller than their own queen. After she has mated, a young queen flies off to start a colony in a new termite mound. Some of the tiny workers go with her, clinging to the hairs on her legs.

A temporary army ant camp or bivouac.

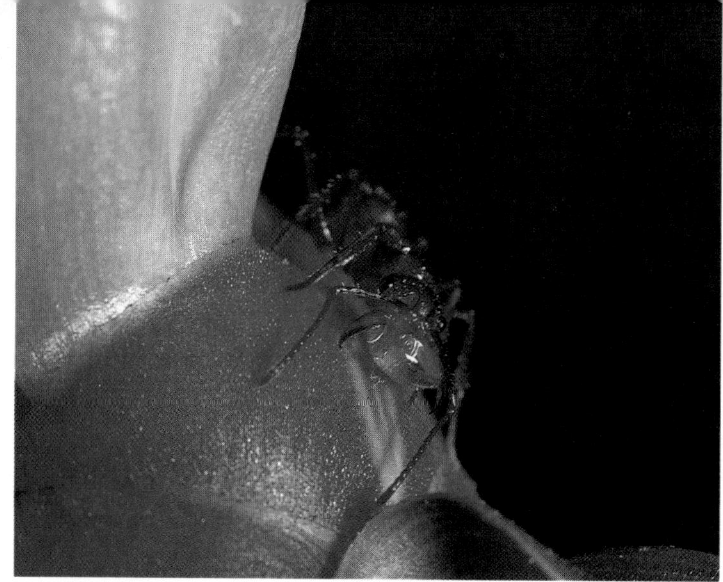

Wild ginger flowers produce nectar which is collected by ants.

Food and feeding

Many ants are vegetarians and feed only on plant material. Some species collect nectar from flowers and the juices from overripe fruit. The ants carry this liquid food back to the nest. Other ants eat pollen and chew flower petals.

If you look closely at some garden plants you may discover the ways in which ants gather liquid food. Any cluster of aphids normally has a group of attendant ants. Aphids feed by piercing the plant stems with their pointed mouthparts to tap the sugary sap. Some of this sap passes straight through the aphid and out of the rear end as droplets of sweet honeydew. Ants find honeydew irresistible, so they stroke the aphids to make them produce more, somewhat like milking cows. The aphids benefit from this relationship because the ants protect their "cows" from *predators* like ladybugs. Many kinds of insects produce honeydew in this way and there are always ants ready to gather it.

The ants on this willow tree are collecting sugary honeydew from aphids.

Leaf-cutters carry off flowers as well as leaves. They hold them over their heads like umbrellas.

In many parts of the world, harvester ants make a living by gathering seeds. Several workers may cooperate to carry larger seeds back to the nest. They store the seeds underground and use them during seasons when other food may be scarce. The ants chew the seeds and mix them with saliva to produce a substance called "ant bread," which is rich in sugars.

In the tropical forests of Central and South America, one of the strangest and yet commonest of sights are the leaf-cutter ants. They are everywhere, in the millions, using their sharp-toothed jaws to bite out small pieces of leaf. They carry these back to their nests, marching in columns, day and night. Each returning worker clutches a piece of leaf in its jaws, held over its back like an umbrella. Indeed, they are sometimes called parasol ants.

Back in the nest, the ants do not eat the leaves. Instead, they chew them up and make a kind of compost, which they store in a moist underground chamber. Here, a special fungus grows on the compost. The ants tend or "garden" the fungus and eat the energy-rich swellings which grow on it. This fungus is found nowhere else in the world. Without the ants, the fungus would not survive, and without the fungus, the leaf-cutter ants would surely starve.

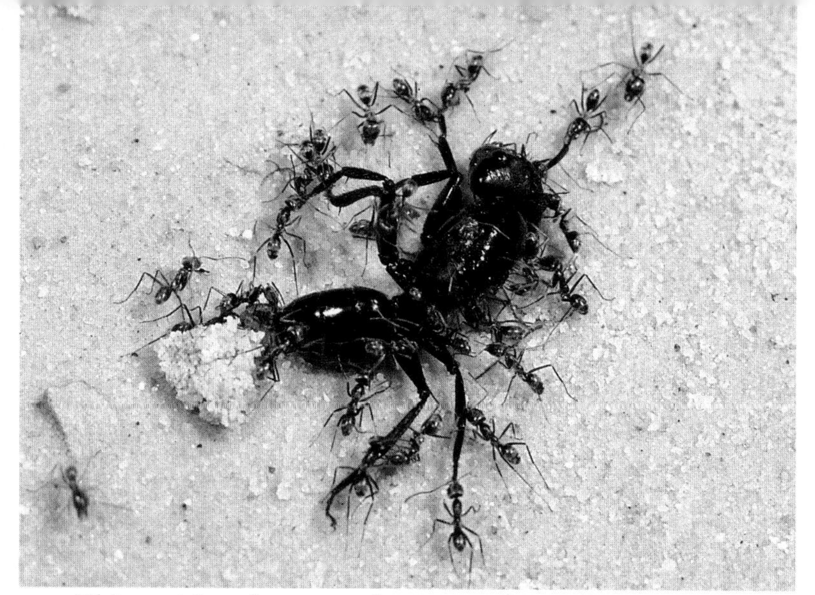

This ant has become the prey of another species.

Predatory or hunting ants

Some ants are predators and feed by killing other animals. Most predatory ants hunt alone, so they can only capture small insects or take pieces of meat from a dead animal. Ants use their senses of smell and sight to find prey. They slowly stalk it, with their antennae carefully folded backward over the head. As they draw near, their jaws open wide and suddenly snap shut on their victims. Ants that have stingers rarely use them to kill food.

If the piece of food is small, the ant carries it back to the nest in a single piece. Food is clasped in the jaws and held over the back between the antennae. An ant with a larger load turns around and drags it backward to the nest. A red ant will sometimes bring back prey weighing four times its own body weight.

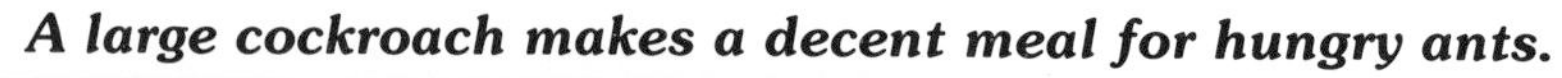

A large cockroach makes a decent meal for hungry ants.

Ants often specialize in just one type of prey, such as caterpillars, worms, wood lice, or springtails. Some will steal the large paralyzed spiders from spider-hunting wasps while the wasps are dragging them back to their own nests. It is quite common for ants to kill and eat the ants from other colonies, or to steal their young. One species of tiny ants lives permanently inside the nest of a larger kind, feeding on their eggs and larvae.

Tropical army ants are blind, yet they are still ferocious hunters. As they move across the forest floor in a seemingly never-ending stream, they capture anything slow or weak in their path. They take mainly other insects and spiders, but will tackle much bigger prey — even the occasional sleeping python or lizard. They will sometimes attack larger animals like horses that are tied up and cannot run away. The ants quickly tear the animal to pieces and carry the food back to a temporary resting place.

Many insects have special ways of protecting themselves from ants. For example, the Cuckoo-spit Bug hides inside a froth of foam, while caterpillars are protected by their hairy coats. Ladybugs survive attack by tucking their legs and antennae in under their smooth, shiny wing cases. The ants eventually give up when they fail to get a grip on the smooth surface. If an ant does manage to grab a leg, the ladybug releases a foul-tasting, sticky yellow liquid through its knee joints. This liquid gums up the ants' antennae and mouthparts.

A wasp grub is carried in a "cradle" of worker ants.

Winged Common Black Ants emerging from the nest.

Mating and egg laying

Toward the end of the season, the old queen in the ant colony makes less and less queen substance. This is a signal for the workers to produce some new queens and males. They feed some of the female larvae with extra food so that they grow into larger queens. When the winged queens hatch out, they stay in the nest until the weather conditions are right. Then they fly off with the males on their "wedding flight."

Before mating, the males get together in groups, often at the tops of tall objects like trees, or on open flat ground. Sometimes they give out a group scent which is attractive to the queens. If an interested queen flies close by, a male will pounce on her and they will mate, either in midair or on the ground. The male transfers sperm from his testes to a special pouch called a *spermatheca*, close to the queen's ovaries. This pouch holds enough sperm to fertilize all the eggs the queen will lay during her lifetime.

A newly emerged wood ant queen with wings still intact.

Now that her wings are not needed any more, the queen sheds them. Later the wing muscles on her body break down. This provides her with a valuable supply of protein which she uses to make her eggs. The queen does not feed until the new ant colony is formed. She has to rely on the food stored within her own body. Some types of queen do not start a new colony right away. Instead they find a crevice to hide in during the winter. They emerge later with the first warm weather of spring to begin egg laying. Other queens start looking for a nesting place as soon as they have mated.

A soil-nesting ant seeks out a patch of bare ground that is warm but not too dry. Here she digs out a small chamber using her jaws. She lays several hundred tiny white bean-shaped eggs. The eggs are the first stage in the life cycle of an ant. They hatch out into larvae that later develop into *pupae* and then into adult ants. As they pass out of her body, the eggs are fertilized by sperm from the spermatheca. The first larvae to hatch eat the rest of the unhatched eggs and develop into workers. They will then build the nest and gather food for the new colony.

A pair of red ants mating.

This queen carpenter ant is guarding her eggs from ground beetles, earwigs, or any other insects looking for an easy meal.

Raising the young

If you open up an ants' nest, you will see many tiny eggs and white larvae or grubs. When disturbed, the worker ants quickly grasp the larvae in their jaws and carry them off to a safer place. In the nest, the workers look after the eggs, constantly licking them and turning them over. This keeps the eggs from drying out, prevents them from getting moldy, and kills *parasites* like mites. When they first hatch, the larvae feed on the yolk of other eggs, which they pierce with their mouthparts. Later the larvae are fed by the workers, who continue to care for them, grooming them and moving them around in the nest. The fat, legless larvae molt or change their skins several times before they turn into slender shiny ants.

Each new skin marks the beginning of a different stage of development called an *instar*. Older larvae smell or feel different from the young larvae, so the workers feed them different foods. Larger, second-instar larvae drink droplets of sweet liquid that the workers *regurgitate* from their crops. If the workers are feeding queen larvae, this liquid may be mixed with a milky fluid containing oil and protein. The workers make this in special head glands.

Yellow Field Ant workers tending their pupae.

The nest of this Black Ant has been disturbed by raising a stone. A worker is moving a pupa to a safe place.

Third-instar larvae can digest fairly large pieces of food. Some predatory ants feed their larvae pieces of meat or dead insects. The workers chew the meat first to help break it down with saliva. Seed-eating ants either chew seeds into smaller pieces for the larvae, or crack the tough outer skin so the larvae can push their heads inside to feed.

When they are fully grown, larvae go into a resting stage called a pupa. Inside the pupa, the body is broken down and rebuilt to form an adult ant. If you break open an early pupa you will find nothing in it but thick yellow liquid! Before it becomes a pupa, the larva wriggles vigorously and pushes off the final larval skin. Underneath is the soft new pupal skin. This skin dries to form a hard, dark shell.

The workers carry the pupae to a warmer, drier part of the nest to complete their development. After a few days, a pale new adult chews its way out of the pupal case. Its exoskeleton darkens as it dries and hardens. This remarkable change from legless larva to an adult is called a complete *metamorphosis*.

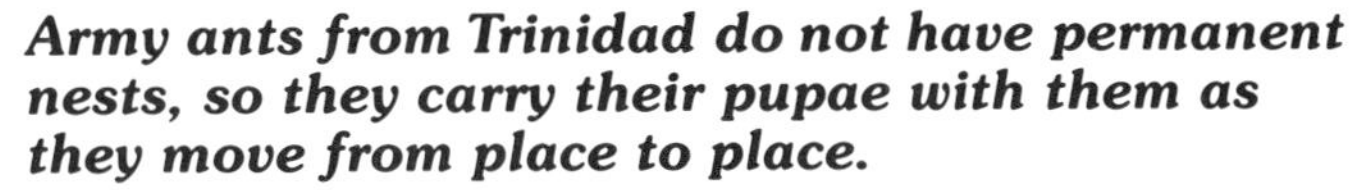

Army ants from Trinidad do not have permanent nests, so they carry their pupae with them as they move from place to place.

Acacia ants collecting sweet nectar from extra-floral nectaries.

Ants and plants

If you ever look closely at a cherry tree, you may notice the two-way traffic of Common Black Ants up and down the trunk. If you follow them upward, you will see them collecting nectar from pairs of tiny red bumps on the leaf stalks. These are called extra-floral nectaries because they produce nectar outside the flower. The tree uses up energy in producing the nectar, but it does gain an advantage — the presence of large numbers of predatory ants that help keep it clear of leaf-eating pests like bugs and caterpillars.

Many other plants allow ants to live on them and some even actively encourage them. Some plants seem to "create" a hollow space deliberately so that an ant colony will make its home in it. As a result, these "ant-plants" are noticeably healthier than surrounding plants because they are free of pests. When grazing animals, like cattle, stop to nibble a leaf or two, the ants swarm all over them and drive them away with painful bites or stings. For the same reason, African farmers leave these ant-plants alone when they are clearing a patch of ground for growing crops.

Thorny Acacia Trees from Africa and South America are typical ant-plants. The base of some of the thorns swells up to form a large, hollow growth. While the tree is still young, a mated queen bites her way through the thorns into the hollow and starts a colony there. The worker ants will attack any insects that dare to land on the tree, even insects many times their own size. The ground at the base of the tree is often littered with dead and crippled insects.

Incredible as it may seem, ants also "garden" around the base of the tree, cutting down young saplings with their sharp jaws. This means that their tree does not become crowded out by other plants. Each acacia has a sizable bare patch of soil around it.

The South American Acacia rewards the ants with "Beltian bodies." They are tiny growths rich in oil and protein that are produced at the leaf tips. The ants collect them for food. The South American Trumpet Tree has a similar association with ants. The center of the tree is hollow, and a single ant colony runs right through it. The ants feed on "Mullerian bodies," special growths that they gather from the base of the leaf stalks.

These leaf-cutter ants from Trinidad are tending their underground fungus garden.

Carpenter ants have a mutually beneficial relationship with the butterfly caterpillar. The caterpillar produces sweet secretions for the ants, while they protect it from enemies.

Ant neighbors and uninvited guests

An ants' nest is a rich source of food, and many animals have learned how to take advantage of it. Some of these uninvited guests actually live inside the nest. Many are scavengers, living on waste or dead material, while others steal the ants' food and young. These intruders have various ways of preventing themselves from being attacked and eaten by the ants.

The caterpillar of the Larke Blue Butterfly, for instance, gets into the nest by fooling the ants into believing that it is an ant larva. When the ant finds the caterpillar, it licks the attractive juices produced from its body.

Australian ants often form special relationships with treehoppers.

This large green caterpillar from Borneo produces secretions that have attracted the attention of some weaver ants.

The caterpillar hunches up its body, which is a signal for the ant to pick it up in its jaws and carry it back to the nest. The caterpillar spends the winter there feeding on ant larvae. Eventually it leaves the nest, changes into a pupa, and then into a beautiful butterfly. If the caterpillar lives in a place where there are no ants of the right kind, it will die.

Many other insects may live in an ants' nest, including beetles, bugs, flies, caterpillars, and wood lice. Some of them are not noticed by the ants because they are very tiny, while others are so similar to ant larvae in smell or shape that they fool the workers into looking after them. They commonly "bribe" the ants by producing sweet liquids from special glands. One rove beetle is so bold that it clings to the queen's abdomen and eats her eggs as she lays them. Another beetle "mugger" attacks adult ants in the narrow passages of the colony and eats them. Even then it is still tolerated in the nest by the other ants.

Several insects use the ants' own communication system against them. For example, a rove beetle persuades a worker ant to part with a droplet of liquid food by tapping it with its antennae. Bristletails just sneak in between two ants that are passing a droplet from mouth to mouth and steal some of it without the ants' noticing.

Sometimes a clever disguise is not enough. The flat white wood louse that is a scavenger in the Common Black Ant nest usually escapes notice because it resembles an ant larva. However, if an ant finds it on its back with its legs in the air, it will attack and kill it.

Anteaters have very long snouts and sticky tongues for extracting ants from their nests.

Ant enemies

Ants have many enemies. They are never safe, either in or out of the nest. Although a single ant does not have much "meat" on it, ants occur in such large numbers that they make a good meal for a hungry predator.

Several mammals have become especially adapted for feeding on ants. The anteaters and Scaly Armadillos of South America and the pangolins of Africa all have large, heavy claws for digging out ant nests and long, sticky tongues for scooping up ants. These animals have poor eyesight and hunt mainly by smell. None of them has any teeth, but the pangolin has a special stomach with a tough, horny lining for crushing ants. The armor plating of the pangolin and the thick skin on its eyelids mean that it is not deterred by any bites or stings. It can also close its nostrils to keep ants from getting up its nose.

Frogs, toads, lizards, and birds like the woodpecker all have long, sticky tongues which they use to snatch a mouthful of ants. A frog can shoot out its tongue, impale an insect, draw it back in, and swallow it all in a fraction of a second.

The ant lion is a fearsome hunter of ants. This ugly creature with huge, sickle-shaped jaws is the larva of the delicate lacewing. The ant lion digs out a smooth-sided, funnel-shaped depression in the sand and then lies in wait at the bottom. Any small insects stumbling into the trap — and ants are by far the most common — slip down the side and cannot climb out again. The ant lion rushes out and devours them.

Several spiders specialize in catching ants, and they wait above the well-worn paths that lead from an ants' nest. The spider drops down silently on a silken thread, catching a lone ant unawares and binding it into a neat parcel. The spider stores its catch until it is hungry and then pierces the ant's skin to suck out the juices.

Like all animals, the ants also have parasites that live either in or on their bodies, feeding on the living tissues. Mites frequently cling to the ant's surface, sucking blood through the soft parts of the exoskeleton. A tiny roundworm sometimes bores through the skin of an ant larva and stays inside its body when it becomes an adult. The worm causes so much damage that the ant does not develop properly.

The ant lion has sickle-shaped jaws for piercing the small insects that fall into its trap.

Protection from enemies

Although ants are small, rather fragile insects, they have a number of weapons which they use to defend themselves and their nests. The Fire Ants of South America, for example, have a very powerful sting, and they often attack people. The poison they inject under the skin produces a burning sensation. If you were unlucky enough to be stung by a lot of these ants, it would make you very ill.

One type of large harvester ant from the Americas uses its sting to protect itself from lizards; it has one of the most powerful insect poisons known, and it can kill a human. The poison spreads around the body, damaging the blood and causing extreme pain. The Common Red Ant of Britain also stings if it feels threatened, but the poison it injects is much weaker and just causes a temporary soreness and itching. If you sat on a nest, however, this would have a longer-lasting effect!

The head of this Australian Bulldog Ant is equipped with toothed jaws that can inflict a painful bite.

The bulldog ant uses its powerful sting both to kill prey and to defend itself.

A mass of Fire Ants floats out across the water, continually rolling over so the insects can breathe.

Bulldog ants from Australia have a nasty combination of large, sharp-toothed jaws and a powerful sting. They take a painful grip on the flesh while thrusting deep into the skin with their stinger. Many ants produce a special scent that tells their nest mates they are in danger. Other ants pick up the signal and rush to help, so the effect of one sting can be multiplied many times. Many ants rely on their bite alone to frighten off their enemies. Larger ants can cause deep wounds — some have such a firm grip that even if their heads are cut off, the jaws stay locked in place! Africans sometimes use the jaws of ants instead of stitches to close large wounds.

A spray of unpleasant or poisonous chemicals can be just as effective as a sting or bite. British wood ants first bite and then release a fine mist of formic acid from the tip of their abdomens; the acid gets into the wound and causes pain.

Doorkeeper Ants have a clever way of keeping intruders out of the nest. The bizarrely shaped worker acts as a living door by blocking the nest entrance hole with an enlarged platelike growth on top of its head. The guard only lets in ants it recognizes. But perhaps the strangest ant of all is the "exploding ant." When it is threatened, its abdomen blows up!

This ant from Costa Rica nests in an Acacia bush. It destroys a young seedling to prevent its competing with the Acacia.

Some ants gather whole flowers for food. This keeps the plant from making seeds.

Ants and people

People have lived with ants for centuries. When archeologists dig up ancient sites, they usually find ant remains among the debris. Quite recently, the Glasshouse Ant — not a native of Britain — was found in a sewer underneath a Roman bathhouse in York, England. It normally lives in warmer Mediterranean countries but it was able to live in the centrally heated homes of the Romans in Britain. It probably traveled to Britain with their baggage. Nowadays, as its name suggests, it is often found in heated greenhouses like those at Kew Gardens in London.

Another world traveler is the Pharaoh's Ant, which normally lives in tropical regions. It is so sensitive to cold that it dies at temperatures below 40°F (4°C). Large buildings like bakeries, hospitals, and cafeterias, which are warm and always have food around, often suffer from infestations of these ants. The ants nest in the channels that carry the heating pipes, so they are very difficult to destroy. Unfortunately, they can easily spread disease in hospitals because they are very fond of flakes of skin and dried blood, so they often forage on used dressings. A modern way of removing them is to give the worker ants food baited with hormones; these hormones prevent the queen from laying normal eggs, so the colony dies out.

Ants are also common in our homes. They are especially attracted to sugar in the kitchen. They are a nuisance, but do little real harm.

Life with ants is not always a battle. In fact, people sometimes use ants for their benefit. Some years ago, cans of chocolate-covered ants began to appear on supermarket shelves, imported from countries where ants are considered a delicacy. The Lapps of northern Finland pack wood ants into a snowball and eat it like a lollipop! But the most useful job ants do is keep down the numbers of pests that damage crops and cause disease. They carry off millions of the eggs and larvae of dirt-loving houseflies, bloodsucking midges, and the mosquitoes that spread the deadly disease malaria. The Chinese have long used weaver ants to protect their lemon trees from insect pests. We know that pesticide sprays damage the environment and scientists are looking at different ways of controlling plant pests, so ants could be very useful. The ants keep away the insects that lay their eggs in flower heads and stop seed production.

Humans have long admired the ant for its tirelessness when gathering and storing food. The illustrations of this French version of the tale of the grasshopper and the ant show the contrasting fates of a lazy cicada who whiles away the summer in song and an industrious ant who prepares for the long winter ahead. Hungry and no longer so devil-may-care, the cicada receives a cold shoulder from the ant in response to its pleas for help.

The ant on the ground

Everywhere you look, from the smallest backyard plot to the largest stretch of forest, you will find ants on the ground, scurrying from place to place in a never-ending search for food. It is not surprising that the Bible holds up the busy ant as an example of the virtues of hard work when it says: "Go to the ant; consider her ways."

Next to plants, ants are probably one of the most important members of the community. But they, too, depend on plants and other animals for food just as still others depend on ants for theirs. These interrelationships built on food are called food chains. This simple diagram shows a food chain involving ants.

Food chain

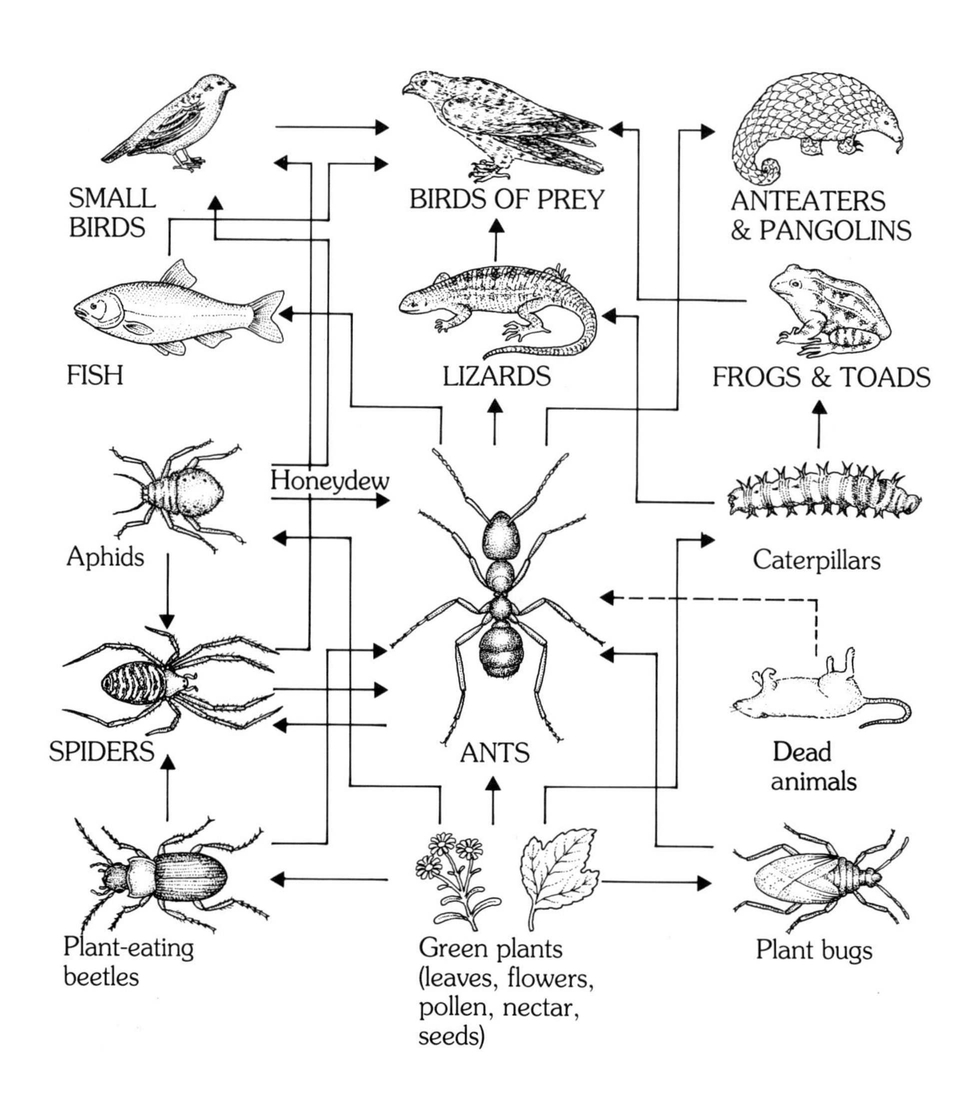

A column of African driver ants spreads out in a never-ending stream across the forest floor.

Plants trap the energy in sunlight and take up minerals and water from the soil. These are passed to the animals which eat the plants. Hunting animals, in turn, gain nutrients from other animals. Dead material also contains valuable nutrients which can be used by scavengers like ants, worms, and wood lice. Eventually all energy is lost to the atmosphere in the form of heat. It is constantly replaced by more energy from sunlight. But minerals are passed from soil to living organisms and back again in a continuous cycle.

If all the ants in the world were removed, a great deal of dead matter would lie around for much longer on the soil surface. The minerals locked up in this waste would only find their way back into the soil very gradually, and plant growth would slow down. Luckily ants, unlike many of the world's animals, are in little danger of becoming extinct. Despite all of the havoc that humans have caused by chopping down forests, flooding valleys, and poisoning the soil, ants have managed to survive. This is partially because most ants are very adaptable and can exploit a wide range of different food sources. Also, they have great powers of reproduction, which means they can rapidly replace any members of the colony that die. So ants will be surviving on or under the ground for many centuries to come.

Glossary and Index

These new words about ants appear in the text on the pages shown after each definition. Each new word first appears in the text in *italics*, just as it appears here.

abdomen ...... third section of an insect's body. **5-8, 23, 27**

antennae ...... two feelers on an ant's head sensitive to touch and smell. **6, 9, 14, 15, 23**

compound eyes .... eyes made of separate sections called facets. **6**

crop .... a special sac in the gut of an ant. **5, 18**

exoskeleton .. tough outer skin to which muscles are attached. **6, 7, 19, 25**

habitat .... place where an animal or plant normally lives. **3, 4**

honeydew ..... mixture secreted by plant-sucking bug. **5, 12**

instar .... one of several stages in insect development. **18, 19**

larva (larvae) . young stage of insect that hatches from egg. **4, 9-11, 15-19, 22, 23, 25, 29**

metamorphosis .... change in body between young and adult stages. **19**

ocelli .... simple, light-sensitive eyes. **6**

ovaries .... structures that make eggs in females. **7, 16**

palps .... short feelers near the mouth used for tasting food. **6**

parasite .... organism that takes its food from living tissues of another organism. **18, 25**

pheromone ... chemical signal released by one animal to affect the behavior of another. **9**

predator .... animal that kills and eats other creatures. **12,14,19,24**

prey .... animal hunted for food by another. **7, 14, 15, 26, 30**

pupa (pupae) . stage in insect life cycle where larval tissues change to adult tissues. **17-19, 23**

queen .... fertile egg-laying female of social wasps, bees, and ants. **7-11, 16-18, 21, 23, 28**

queen substance ..... chemical secreted by queen to prevent production of new queens by workers. **8**

regurgitate .... to bring food back into the mouth from the stomach before digestion and pass it out of the body. **18**

species .... a particular kind of animal or plant. **2, 4, 6, 7, 9-12,14,15**

sperm .... male sex cells that are used to fertilize a female's egg. **7, 16, 17**

spermatheca . sac in female where sperm is stored after mating. **16, 17**

thorax .... middle section of body. **6, 7**

workers .... sterile female insects that do all the work. **4-11, 13, 16-19, 21, 23, 27, 28**

Reading level analysis: FRY 5, FLESCH 83 (easy), RAYGOR 6, FOG 6
Library of Congress Cataloging-in-Publication Data
Losito, Linda.
The ant on the ground / words by Linda Losito ; photographs by Oxford Scientific Films.
p. cm. -- (Animal habitats)
Summary: Text and photographs depict ants in their natural habitats, illustrating how they feed, defend themselves, and breed.
ISBN 0-8368-0111-3
1. Ants--Juvenile literature. [1. Ants.] I. Oxford Scientific Films. II. Title. III. Series.
QL568.F7L67 1989
595.79'6--dc20 89-4460

North American edition first published in 1989 by Gareth Stevens, Inc., 7317 West Green Tree Road, Milwaukee, WI 53223, USA

Conceived, designed, and produced by Belitha Press Ltd., London.
Consultant Editor: Jennifer Coldrey. Art Director: Treld Bicknell. Design: Naomi Games. US Editor: Mark J. Sachner. Line Drawings: Lorna Turpin.

The publishers wish to thank the following for permission to reproduce copyright material: **Oxford Scientific Films Ltd.** for title page, pp. 8 both, 11, 14 below, 16 below, 18 both, 19 below, 21, 22 below, 29 (J. A. L. Cooke); pp. 2, 12 below (D. R. Specker); p. 3 (Barrie Watts); p. 4 (Waina Cheng); pp. 5 above, 10, 26 right (Mantis Wildlife Films); p. 5 below (Densey Clyne); p. 6 (G. I. Bernard); p. 7 above (Raymond Mendez); pp. 7 below, 9, 28 right (OSF); front cover, p. 12 above (Gerald Thompson); p. 13 (Richard K. LaVal); p. 14 above (Alastair Shay); p. 15 (M. P. L. Fogden); pp. 16 above, 19 above (Peter O'Toole); p. 17 (Tim Shepherd); pp. 20, 28 left (Philip Sharpe); p. 22 above (David Thompson); p. 24 (Breck P. Kent); p. 25 (Wallace Kirkland); p. 26 left (Kathie Atkinson); p. 27 (C. C. Lockwood); p. 31 (P. & W. Ward); back cover (Animals Animals — George K. Bryce); Partridge Productions for p. 23.

Printed in the United States of America
1 2 3 4 5 6 7 8 9 95 94 93 92 91 90 89